ENGLISH ELECTRIC DIESEL LOCOMOTIVES

George Woods

AMBERLEY

First published 2020

Amberley Publishing
The Hill, Stroud
Gloucestershire, GL5 4EP

www.amberley-books.com

Copyright © George Woods, 2020

The right of George Woods to be identified as the
Author of this work has been asserted in
accordance with the Copyrights, Designs and
Patents Act 1988.

ISBN 978 1 3981 0191 3 (print)
ISBN 978 1 3981 0192 0 (ebook)

British Library Cataloguing in Publication Data.
A catalogue record for this book is available from
the British Library.

Typeset in 9.5pt on 12pt Celeste.
Origination by Amberley Publishing.
Printed in the UK.

Introduction

This is the first of a series of books on BR diesel and electric locos and shows some of the English Electric designs that helped to eliminate steam traction in the 1960s and which paved the way for a very different railway into the 1970s and beyond.

The English Electric company came into existence in 1918 after the end of the First World War, with the merging of many small companies that were manufacturing locomotives, aircraft, diesel engines and electrical machines, both for industrial and domestic use.

After purchasing Dick Kerr & Co. and its Preston works in 1919, it then gained the ability to build trams and trolleybuses for many British operators, and was also able to enter the overseas market.

At first business was good, but with the advent of the Wall Street Crash of 1929 the company had to make many changes and it was not until 1933 that business improved, and it was 1936 before English Electric became profitable enough to pay its first dividend since 1924.

With the construction of its first electric locomotives in 1923 for service in New Zealand, it then became a major manufacturer of locomotives and electrical parts for railway electrification schemes both at home and overseas, including the Southern Railway electrification in the 1930s.

The first diesel loco was built in 1936 at the former Dick Kerr works in Preston and diesel locos were produced here until English Electric took over the Vulcan Foundry at Newton le Willows in 1955, which then became the main locomotive works. It remained the major British manufacturer of diesel and electric locomotives until the takeover of English Electric in 1968 by GEC, which resulted in the end of locomotive construction in 1970.

With the exception of shunters, very little interest was shown in diesel locos by the British railway companies in the 1930s, but after the end of the Second World War the advantages of diesels over steam were becoming more apparent, as shown by the success of diesel traction in the USA.

EE had developed several engines that powered locos which were sold in many countries worldwide, and in 1946 its 1,600 hp engine was used in two prototype diesel electric locos, Nos 10000/10001, for the LMS which were built at Derby and which entered service just before Britain's railways were nationalised in 1948. Soon after, three more powerful locos of 1,750 hp, Nos 10201/2, and 2,000 hp No. 10203, ordered by the Southern Railway, were built at Ashford and Brighton Works, which after some teething problems successfully entered service in 1950–54. All five remained in service until around the mid-1960s.

When British Railways announced its Modernisation Scheme in 1955, which aimed to eliminate steam power by the mid-1970s, EE received orders for twenty 1,000 hp locomotives for local freight duties, and ten 2,000 hp locomotives for express passenger and long-distance freight work, which entered service in 1957 and 1958.

It soon became apparent that 2,000 hp was no great advance in power over the steam locomotives to be replaced, and that something like 3,000 hp was needed to speed up services to the extent required. EE then developed a 3,300 hp loco which used two 1,650 hp high-speed Napier *Deltic* engines, originally used to power motor torpedo boats. A prototype known as the Deltic entered service in 1958 and soon produced some impressive speed and load haulage feats which were way above that of any of the locos then in service. This did not prevent BR ordering a total of 200 of the 2,000 hp locos, which eventually became Class 40; they proved very popular and reliable in everyday service on secondary passenger and freight trains, and lasted until 1985.

The Eastern Region of BR saw that electrification of the ECML would not even begin until the WCML electrification was finished in 1966; in fact, because of political delays the ECML was not electrified fully until 1991. It was decided to order twenty-two Deltics as a stopgap to speed up the majority of their long-distance services until the electrification could be finished. They would be assisted by the 2,750 hp Brush Class 47 locomotives, which came into service in the mid-1960s. The Deltics entered service in 1961–62 and revolutionised ECML services. The Flying Scotsman had its journey time from King's Cross to Edinburgh reduced from over 7 hours to 6 hours, and other Anglo-Scottish and West Yorkshire services also saw large reduction in journey times. They continued in service until the introduction of the InterCity 125 in 1978 made them redundant, and were taken out of service by the end of 1981.

In 1959 a smaller version of the Deltic was built, powered by a single Deltic engine. Unfortunately, these Baby Deltic locos were never a success and, despite receiving replacement engines, they were withdrawn from service by 1971.

The 1,000 hp locos which became Class 20 were very successful and 288 eventually came into service, especially after alternative locos built for similar duties by other manufacturers proved so unreliable that they were scrapped after a few years in service. Fifty years after their introduction, some Class 20s are still in daily service with Direct Rail Services and can be seen on light freight duties in many parts of the country.

A further need was for a medium-powered mixed traffic loco, and EE introduced the 1,750 hp Type 3, which became Class 37, a total of 309 of which were built between 1959 and 1964. Very similar in looks to the Class 40, they became the BR workhorse, seeing service on both passenger and freight duties all over the system, and a good number remain in service today with several freight operators.

In 1962 a prototype 2,700 hp loco, DP2, was introduced, and proved extremely successful, so in 1967–68 fifty locos which became Class 50 came into service on the WCML to speed up the Anglo-Scottish services north of Crewe. They were used in pairs to provide enough power for the steep gradients in Cumbria and Scotland. The original DP2 design was improved in many ways but many of these so-called improvements proved problematic in service. When the electrification of the WCML was extended from Crewe to Glasgow in 1974, the Class 50s were transferred to the Western Region to replace the last of their diesel-hydraulics and, after a major refurbishment, settled down to give good service to the West Country from both Paddington and Waterloo, but after the introduction of the 125s, they were gradually taken out of service by 1994.

Last but not least was the original EE 0-6-0 diesel shunter, first introduced in 1935 and built jointly with Hawthorn Leslie for the LMS, SR, GWR and LNER. This design was developed into the BR Class 08/09, which became the principle BR shunting loco, and more than 1,000 were built between 1952 and 1962. Some remain in service today, not only on preserved railways but also with many TOCs, which still find them very useful.

Of all the companies that built locos during the BR modernisation period, EE-built locomotives have proved to be some of the most reliable and long-lived, as the number that are still in service today goes to prove.

Abbreviations

BR	British Railways
CP	Caminhos de Ferro Portugueses (Portuguese Railways)
DRS	Direct Rail Services
ECML	East Coast Main Line
EE	English Electric
EEVF	English Electric Vulcan Foundry
GEC	General Electric Company
GWR	Great Western Railway
LMS	London, Midland & Scottish Railway
LNER	London & North Eastern Railway
RSH	Robert Stephenson Hawthorns
SR	Southern Railway
TOC	Train Operating Company
VF	Vulcan Foundry
WCML	West Coast Main Line

Looking very smart in Load Haul livery is this fine example of English Electric motive power. No. 50135 *Ark Royal* is seen at the Eastleigh Works Centenary exhibition on 25 May 2009.

Rhodesia Railways DE2 No. 1207 calls at Plumtree station on 24 September 1973 with the daily Bulawayo to Mafeking (South Africa) train. Soon after departure it will cross the border into Botswana. No. 1207 was one of twenty-three locos built by English Electric in 1955 at the Dick Kerr Works in Preston, and another twelve were built at VF. They were fitted with the EE 16SVT 1,750 hp engine, which was similar to those used in LMS No. 10000/1 and the BR Class 37 and Class 40.

Still in its original blue livery, Combois de Portugal CP 101 No. 1410 leaves Contimul Yard near Porto, on 14 April 1974, with a freight bound for Barca De Alva via the Douro Valley line. No. 1410 was one of ten locos built at EEVF in 1967, and a further fifty-seven locos were built under license in Portugal by Sorefame at their Lisbon works. They were based on the BR Class 20 but fitted with an engine uprated to 1,370 hp. Ten were later sold on to Argentina Railways.

D3735 is about to leave Inverness Harbour on 14 October 1971 with an empty diesel tank wagon. Built at Crewe works in 1959, this loco is still shown as in service today as No. 08568.

Nos 08276–712 were used as station pilots at Perth, and are in between duties at the west side of the station on 27 May 1977.

D8026 and a sister loco pass through Backworth with coal empties on 9 May 1969. D8026 was based at Gateshead at this time and was built by RSH and scrapped at MC Metals, Springburn, in 1991.

Taken from a passing train, a wonderful variety of 1970s diesel power, including No. 20040, is seen in this photograph of Derby MPD in April 1976. Also in the picture can be seen examples of Classes 24 and 47.

No. 20209 and another Class 20 pass Rotherham Masborough station on 9 June 1977 with a trainload of steel. No. 20209 was built at EEVF in 1967 and scrapped at Michael Douglas Ltd, Carlisle, in 2001. The station closed in 1988 after the more centrally sited Rotherham Central station was opened.

No. 20021 passes through York station in May 1981 with two empty vans for the nearby Rowntree chocolate factory. No. 20021 was built at RSH in 1959 and scrapped at MC Metals, Springburn, in 1992.

Nos 20129 and 20011 come off the Sheffield line at Bridge Junction, Doncaster, heading a very mixed freight for the nearby Belmont Yard in October 1981.

Nos 20061, 20093 and 47444 pass Blea Moor on 25 November 1989 with the afternoon Carlisle to Leeds train. For several Saturdays at this time BR ran the morning Leeds to Carlisle and the return afternoon service using unusual motive power, which attracted enthusiasts to swell the number of passengers.

With both locos wearing Railfreight large logo grey livery, Nos 20132 and 20010 pass Strensall on the York to Scarborough line on 12 December 1990 with the Class 20 Loco Society Vladivostok Avoider railtour from Sheffield to Scarborough and return. No. 20132 was built at EEVF in 1966 and is still in service with Harry Needles Ltd. No. 20010 was built in 1957 and scrapped at MC Metals, Springburn, in 1994.

Nos 20059 and 20168 near Ulverston on 25 April 1992 with the 15.32 from Barrow to Preston. On this day Regional Railways, in conjunction with Pathfinder Tours, ran several Lancastrian mini excursions, partly using service trains, with unusual motive power. The train is passing Plumpton Junction, and the tankers are waiting to go down the branch to the Glaxochem works. In the background on the hill is the Hoad Monument, which was built to resemble a lighthouse.

On one of the first railtours to utilise DRS power after the company was formed in 1995, Nos 20304 and 20305 pass Shipton on the ECML with Pathfinder's Geordie Choppers railtour. The tour ran from Bristol to Newcastle and return on 14 September 1996.

DRS No. 20301 *Max Joule 1955–1999* and No. 20302 wait at Carlisle station on their way to the nearby DRS maintenance depot at Kingmoor on 10 June 2003.

DRS No. 20905 at Doncaster Works open day on 26 July 2003. Now owned by Harry Needle & Co., it is on hire to GB Railfreight.

D8000, now preserved as part of the National collection at York, is seen at the York Railway Festival on 31 May 2004. This was the first EE Type 1, built in 1957, and also the first diesel loco built for the BR Modernisation Scheme.

In Railfreight triple grey livery, No. 20031 is seen at Keighley station on the Keighley & Worth Valley Railway on 14 June 2007. It has been at the KWVR since it was withdrawn by BR in 1990.

DRS Nos 20303 and 20304 are seen in wintry conditions near Ormside on the Settle & Carlisle line with the Fellsman Chopper railtour, which ran from Birmingham to Carlisle and return on 7 February 2009.

DRS Nos 20302 and 20303 approach Hutton Cranswick station on the Hull to Scarborough line with the rail head treatment train, bound for Bridlington on 21 October 2015.

Baby Deltic D5906 passes Hadley Wood station on 21 October 1966 with an outer suburban train from King's Cross to Baldock. The van at the front of the train was used to take soiled tablecloths and sheets, etc. from restaurant and sleeping cars to the British Transport Hotels laundry at Baldock.

Another Baby Deltic, D5905, passes Harringay West station on 17 February 1969 with a train for King's Cross. The remains of the burnt-out booking office can be seen on the footbridge; it was set alight by thieves after the day's takings. As this station was far from being the busiest on the GN suburban system, they must have gone away very disappointed.

D6706 passes Hadley Wood station on 21 October 1966 with a tanker train from Royston to Ripple Lane. There used to be a bottleneck through here as far as Potters Bar until 1959, when the work to add another two tracks through the station and three tunnels was finished.

D6710 is about to back into the yard to pick up a train of coal empties at Rose Grove on 1 May 1968. At this time D6710 was allocated to Healey Mills and has worked here on a coal train from the Yorkshire pits.

D6868 climbs into Rose Grove on 13 July 1968 with coal empties from Padiham power station to Healey Mills yard. A Class 8F gives rear-end assistance.

D6876 approaches Radyr with a coal train on the Penarth line as No. 6991 passes, heading light engine towards Cardiff docks, on 22 July 1969.

No. 6865 glints in the setting sun as it approaches South Tottenham station with empty cement wagons for Purfleet in October 1969.

No. 6723 crosses Dinting viaduct on 11 November 1969 with the Manchester Piccadilly to Harwich boat train. The fifth vehicle was one of the few remaining Gresley buffet cars.

No. 6865 passes New Barnet station on 16 December 1969 with a train of empty oil tankers heading for the refinery at Thameshaven.

Taken from a St Pancras to Sheffield train, No. 6783 is seen approaching Clay Cross South Junction on 30 December 1969 with a coal train bound for Toton Yard.

D6805 passes through Penistone station on a cold and snowy 30 December 1969 with a short westbound freight.

D6968 arrives at Penistone station on 30 December 1969 with the Harwich to Manchester Piccadilly boat train. These services connected with the overnight sailings to and from the Hook of Holland.

No. 6725 heads east through Stratford station on 12 September 1970 with a train of empty sand hoppers from Mile End to Southminster.

The late afternoon sun catches No. 6835 as it passes the site of Marshfield (Mon) station, which closed in 1959, with an eastbound freight.

A short time later No. 6921 passes with a westbound train on 4 April 1973. The Western Region used a very fierce cleaner in their loco washing plants at this time, which not only removed the dirt but much of the paint as well.

No. 6902 is just about visible through the murk as it passes Maesteg on 5 April 1973 with a short train of loaded coal wagons from the local colliery.

No. 37027, which was based at March depot at this time, is seen arriving at York station on 10 July 1976 with a train from Yarmouth.

No. 37144 departs from Gleneagles station on 27 May 1977 with a Glasgow to Dundee train.

No. 37037 is deputising for a Class 47 as it waits to leave Liverpool Street station on 4 July 1977 with a train for Norwich.

No. 37279 outside Doncaster Works on 18 June 1978. It is on accommodation bogies to allow the locomotive body to be transported between workshops.

No. 37089 heads out of London on the slow line, passing Southall MPD with a train of oil tankers on 1 March 1979.

Two Class 37s near Tollerton on the ECML with a southbound Merry Go Round coal train bound for one of the Yorkshire power stations. This photograph was taken in December 1979.

No. 37115 passes Shipton on the ECML with a summer Saturday Scarborough to Glasgow train in July 1981.

An unidentified Class 37 stands alongside the ex-North Eastern Railway overall roof at Malton station in August 1981, with the Scarborough to York pick-up freight. The overall roof was removed in 1989, but the station remains unusual because of its single platform face serving trains in both directions.

No. 37195 passes Shipton with the Doncaster Works test train in October 1981. This set of parcels vans was used for test runs with locos that had just been overhauled at Doncaster Works.

No. 37063 at York Holgate in August 1982. The loco is freshly painted after a recent overhaul at Doncaster.

No. 37107 waits to leave Ely station with a train from Liverpool Street to Kings Lynn in July 1983. The scene here was transformed with the electrification from Liverpool Street to Kings Lynn in 1992.

No. 37183 crosses a train from Kyle of Lochalsh at Achnasheen station with the morning Inverness to Kyle of Lochalsh train in October 1983.

No. 37037 arrives at Oban station, passing the large Caledonian Railway signal box with a train from Glasgow Queen Street in October 1983.

No. 37026 *Loch Awe* waits at a diesel-fume-filled Glasgow Queen Street station with the afternoon train for Fort William in October 1983.

No. 37064 leaves a busy York Dringhouses yard with a southbound freight in October 1983, with a Class 47 waiting to follow with another freight. The yard was closed in the late 1980s, and a housing estate now occupies the site.

A rare sighting of a Class 37 on the Settle & Carlisle line, as No. 37095 passes Horton in Ribblesdale station with the 15.55 Leeds to Carlisle train on 4 May 1985. The signal cabin here was opened in 1875, closed in 1984, and was destroyed by fire on 24 April 1991.

No. 37170 passes Colton Junction with a very mixed Speedlink freight heading towards York in June 1986.

The wonderful display of rhododendrons at Glenfinnan station makes a colourful backdrop to the arrival of No. 37404 *Ben Cruachan* in Large Logo livery with a Fort William to Mallaig train.

Shortly after No. 37405 *Strathclyde Region* departs for Fort William with the morning train from Mallaig on 24 June 1986.

Still in Scotland, No. 37056 passes more rhododendrons at Loch Awe station on 25 June 1986 with a short freight from Oban heading towards Crianlarich. The station was closed in 1965 but reopened in 1985.

Nos 37178 and 47431 pass Kirkby Stephen station on 2 May 1987 with the newspaper empty vans from Stranraer to Redbank sidings in Manchester. This train was diverted over the S&C as the WCML was closed for engineering works.

No. 37043 waits in the loop at Taynauilt, to pass a train from Oban, on 23 September 1987, with a train of fuel for the Macbraynes ships which sail from Oban to the outlying islands.

No. 37502 *British Steel Teesside* and No. 37501 *Teesside Steelmaster* have stopped in the sidings at York Holgate for a crew change before continuing to the British Steel works at Middlesbrough. This photograph was taken in April 1988.

Nos 37687 and 37688 *Great Rocks* in Construction Sector livery, at Buxton TMD in July 1989. These locos were used on aggregate trains serving the quarries in the Peak District.

No. 37430 *Cwymbran* in InterCity Mainline livery passes Weston Rhyn on 12 October 1990 with the Castle Cement train from Penyffordd to Oakengates.

No. 37223, seen here in Coal Sector livery, heads north through York station with a train of Russells coal containers in October 1991.

No. 37418 *Pectinidae*, in Petroleum Sector livery, has just crossed Levens viaduct and is approaching Ulverston on 25 April 1992 with a Regional Railways train from Preston to Barrow.

No. 37003, in Dutch livery, prepares to leave the loop alongside Berwick-upon-Tweed station with a wagon load of pipes in August 1992.

No. 37421 *The Kingsman*, in Regional Railways livery, has just left Cowburn Tunnel and is approaching Edale on with a Hope Valley Centenarian Special train on 26 June 1994.

No. 37211 at South Milford on 27 April 1996 with a train of Cawood coal containers from the Selby mine to Seaforth (Liverpool) for onward shipping to Northern Ireland.

No. 37798, in Mainline livery, heads west past the site of Brent station on 12 July 1996 with a train of tanks, probably containing diesel fuel for Plymouth Laira TMD. Brent was the junction for the Kingsbridge branch, which was closed on 16 September 1963. Brent station closed soon after on 5 October 1964.

No. 37059 *Port of Tilbury* in Distribution livery and No. 37058 run downhill through Birkett Common on 20 July 1996 with the Settle Syphons railtour from King's Cross to Carlisle and return.

No. 37711, in Metals Sector livery, near Gascoigne Wood on 17 March 1997 with the Mostyn (Flintshire) to Hull acetic acid tanks.

No. 37667 *Meldon Quarry Centenary* in EWS livery and No. 47710 *Quasimodo* in Waterman Railways livery wait at Carlisle station with the return leg of the Past Time Tours First and Last railtour, which ran from King's Cross on 28 June 1997.

No. 37196 crosses over onto the fast line at Colton Junction in July 1998 while heading a northbound freight.

No. 37203 heads a rail head treatment train towards Scarborough at York Haxby on 15 October 1999 with another Class 37 at the rear.

No. 37521 *English China Clay* and No. 37682 *Hartlepool Pipe Mill* head for Scarborough via Hull, past Colton Junction, with the 'Pathfinders Napier Navigator' railtour on 6 April 2002.

No. 37197 in Ian Riley Engineering livery passes Darnholme on the North Yorkshire Moors Railway during a diesel weekend on 11 April 2003. No. 37197 was owned by Ian Riley at this time, but he later sold it to DRS, where it remained in service until it was scrapped in 2012.

No. 37418 *East Lancashire Railway* is seen on 14 June 2003 in the siding at Fort William station, coupled to the sleeping cars that will form the overnight West Highlander service to London Euston.

No. 37401 *The Royal Scotsman* passes a service train at Glenfinnan station on 16 April 2003. It is heading the Royal Scotsman luxury train from Mallaig to Fort William.

No. 37405 waits at Appleby station on 13 October 2003 with the afternoon train from Carlisle to York, which for a period was worked with a Class 37 at each end.

No. 37516, in Loadhaul livery, passes York Towthorpe on 15 November 2003 with the rail head treatment train, returning from Scarborough. Another Loadhaul Class 37 is on the rear of the train.

Just before 7 a.m., No. 37411 *The Scottish Railway Society* is seen waiting to leave York station on 2 June 2004 at the rear of the service to Carlisle via Harrogate and Leeds.

No. 37901 *Mirlees Pioneer*, in grey large logo livery, is seen at the Llangollen Railway MPD on 15 September 2006. In 1986 No. 37901 was one of the Class 37s rebuilt with a 1,800 hp Mirrlees engine and after its time in preservation is now owned by Europhoenix and is back on the main line.

No. 37610 *Ted Cassady*, in DRS livery, with No. 37606 at the rear, is seen approaching Ais Gill summit on 30 September 2006 with the Network Rail Ultrasonic Test Train.

Nos 37087 and 37261 at Appleby station on 3 October 2006 with the rail head treatment train from Carlisle.

Nos 37218 and 20303 waiting for the green signal at Carlisle station on 23 February 2007 with a nuclear flask for Sellafield in tow.

No. 37676 *Loch Rannoch*, in West Coast Railways livery, passes Keld Farm on 6 December 2008 with a special train running south over the Settle & Carlisle line.

West Coast Railways Nos 37706 and 37516 look resplendent, while EWS No. 37411(D6990) *Castell Caerffili*, owned at the time by EWS but repainted in BR Green, is looking a bit work-stained. All three are seen at the Eastleigh Works Open Day on 25 May 2009. No. 37411 was scrapped in May 2013.

Two immaculate DRS Class 37s, Nos 37259 and 37425 *Sir Robert McAlpine*, arrive at Appleby station on 11 April 2014, with the special train which marked the twenty-fifth anniversary of the saving of the Settle & Carlisle line from closure. No. 37409 was at the rear.

Colas Rail Nos 37219 and 37175 depart northwards from the sidings alongside Doncaster station on 7 July 2015 with a Network Rail test train.

Euro Phoenix Rail No. 37608 *Andromeda* is seen at the Crewe Open Day on 8 June 2019. This loco was purchased from DRS in 2016 and is currently one of eight Class 37s owned by the company.

An unidentified Class 40 passes Hadley Wood on 21 October 1966 with a southbound fast freight bound for the King's Cross freight terminal.

Another unidentified Class 40 passes under the Greenholme road bridge while heading a southbound freight down from Shap summit on the foggy morning of 18 November 1967.

A Class 40 passes the site of Brock station, which closed back in 1939, with a southbound passenger train on 24 February 1968.

A Class 40-hauled freight slogs up the hill out of Brinnington tunnel on 30 April 1968. It includes an ex-LMS diesel shunter making its last journey to a scrap yard. The train is on the now-closed Stockport Tiviot Dale to Woodley Junction line.

D244 approaches Woodley Junction on 4 May 1968 with a train of Ford Escorts which are fresh from the Ford plant at Halewood near Liverpool. Note the lovely old Midland Railway signal controlling the exit from the goods sidings.

Class 40 D265 passes through Finsbury Park station with a lengthy express, just 2 miles from its destination at King's Cross, on 17 February 1969. This busy station was in a near derelict state at this time but was extensively rebuilt for the GN electrics, which started running in 1976.

No. 290 comes off of the Stalybridge line at Guide Bridge West Junction on 11 November 1969 with a coal train from the Yorkshire pits bound for the Manchester area.

Seen on a quiet Sunday morning, No. 40167 is one of about half a dozen diesels stabled on the middle road at Carlisle station in March 1976.

No. 281 is standing in the loco yard at King's Cross station in April 1972, along with a selection of Eastern diesels. The scene has been completely transformed: first by electrification in the mid-1970s, after which the loco yard closed in 1979, and recently the site has been used for an office block.

No. 40173 crosses the Royal Border Bridge at Berwick-upon-Tweed on 12 July 1976 with a Haverton Hill to Grangemouth train of anhydrous ammonia tanks.

No. 40153 departs from Markinch station and passes the North British Railway signal box with a local train for Edinburgh Waverley on 27 May 1977.

No. 40088 approaches Markinch with a Freightliner service from Aberdeen on 27 May 1977.

No. 40056 approaches Gleneagles, with the Ochil Hills as a backdrop, while heading a Glasgow to Dundee express on 27 May 1977.

No. 40101 crosses the layout to Platform 2 as it arrives at Perth station with a train for Dundee on 27 May 1977.

No. 40184 leaves Inverkeithing and starts the climb to the Forth Bridge with a train for Edinburgh on 28 May 1977. The line disappearing to the right of the picture goes to the James Wright scrapyard, which disposed of many steam locomotives in the 1960s.

No. 40107 passes Guide Bridge station with an eastbound empty hopper train on 9 June 1977. The steeple of St Stephen's Church dominates the background. This once busy junction, which saw long-distance trains from Manchester to Marylebone stopping, has been reduced from four platforms to two since reorganisation of the track layout in 1984.

No. 40020 takes the Stockport line as it approaches Guide Bridge station with a breakdown train on 9 June 1977.

No. 40023 is about to pass through Rotherham Masborough station on the line towards Chesterfield with a southbound freight in September 1977.

No. 40071 has just arrived in Platform 1 at King's Cross station with a relief train from the north in August 1978. The roof is undergoing cleaning and renovation as part of the station improvements and the electrification of the suburban services.

A group of enthusiasts look on as the driver of No. 40119 waits for the right away at York station with a train for Scarborough in September 1979.

No. 40073 leaves York Yard North with a southbound freight in December 1979. In the 1970s York was quite a busy industrial centre, with the British Sugar Corporation works in the background adding to the murk.

With the slopes of Wild Boar Fell in the background, No. 40109 climbs the last few yards to the 1,169-foot Ais Gill summit with a southbound freight in May 1980.

No. 40106 with Nos 26020 and 86214 in tow at the Rainhill Cavalcade on 25 May 1980. No. 40106 was withdrawn in 1983 but is now preserved in working order, No. 26020 is now an exhibit at the NRM in York, and No. 86214 was withdrawn and scrapped in 2006.

No. 40135 passes Shipton with a lengthy northbound relief express on a wet June day in 1981. Even after the introduction of InterCity 125s in 1978 it was still possible to see Class 40s on relief trains, especially on summer Saturdays.

It was a white Christmas in 1981, and No. 40106 is seen in this icy view at York MPD on Boxing Day.

No. 40068 waits in the middle road at York station with a southbound empty stock train in June 1982.

No. 40185 makes a cautious approach to Skipton station with a Ministry of Defence freight from the M.O.D. depot at Warcop, probably heading for the naval dockyard at Plymouth with a load of ordnance in July 1982.

No. 40169 at York TMD in February 1983. This loco was unusual as the steam-heating boiler water tank had been removed, leaving a sizeable gap between the bogies.

Two views of No. 40152, which was pressed into service on diverted WCML services via the Settle & Carlisle line because of engineering works on 2 April 1983. The first view shows the southbound Royal Scot approaching Shotlock Hill Tunnel, and in the second No. 40152 heads away from the Ribblehead viaduct with the northbound Royal Scot. The passengers on both these trains will be feeling the cold as Class 40s were not equipped with electric train heating.

No. 40129 stands at Blea Moor on standby loco duties on 2 April 1983. This loco was one of twenty-two produced with split headcode boxes.

No. 40035 waits in Platform 9 at York station and then departs for Scarborough on a Sunday morning in April 1983. York station, which opened in 1877, is reckoned to be one of the finest stations on Britain's railways and, apart from damage sustained from bombing in 1942, has survived in largely original condition.

No. 40168 passes Leeds station with a Glazebrook to Haverton Hill tanker train in September 1984.

Nos 40181 and D200 head up the ECML near Tollerton with the Hertfordshire Railtours Tees Tyne Boggard tour from King's Cross to Newcastle and return on 27 October 1984.

Nos 40152 and 40086 pass Greenholme on the climb to Shap summit with the RESL Royal Scot railtour from Euston to Glasgow and return on 28 December 1984.

D200 passes a busy looking Dringhouses Yard on 9 March 1985 with the Whistler Finale railtour from York to London Liverpool Street and return.

D200 climbs away from Horton in Ribblesdale with the afternoon service from Leeds to Carlisle on 3 May 1986. The picture was taken during the infamous storm which came over from Chernobyl, of which the rain was said to be polluted by radioactive fallout. My wife says I have never been the same since!

D200 arrives at York with the Class 40 Farewell railtour from London Liverpool Street station to York on 16 April 1988. This was the final journey made by the locomotive before it went into the NRM at York.

No. 40145 on display at the Crewe Works open day on 10 September 2005. The loco is in the care of the Class 40 Preservation Society and is currently at Barrow Hill under repair.

D401 has the attention of local enthusiasts as it waits to leave a very gloomy Preston station on 29 April 1968 with a northbound express.

D413 runs through pleasant country near Bolton le Sands with a southbound Freightliner train on 15 July 1968.

An unidentified Class 50 departs from Carnforth station on 11 July 1968 with a Carlisle to London Euston train that will combine at Preston with a portion from Blackpool.

D426 passes Carnforth with a southbound Freightliner train on 11 July 1968. There are quite a lot of steam locomotives at work in the background considering that only about three weeks remain before the end of BR steam on 4 August 1968.

D409 arrives at Lancaster with an extremely varied rake of vans on a northbound parcels train on 15 July 1968.

D417 crosses the Lune Bridge to the north of Lancaster station on 15 July 1968 with through coaches for Barrow which have come from London Euston.

D442 is passing Shap Wells on the climb to the 916-foot Shap summit with a northbound Freightliner train on 26 October 1968.

A Class 50 roars south through Tebay station with a Glasgow to Euston train in September 1968. Tebay station closed on 1 July 1968 along with many of the other wayside stations on the WCML north of Preston.

No. 419 arrives at Penrith station with the afternoon train from Carlisle to Euston on 4 March 1972. Later the same day, Nos 421 and 448 pass through Penrith with the northbound Royal Scot Euston to Glasgow Central express. This was the last day of services on the much missed Penrith to Keswick line.

Nos 438 and 422 await departure time at Carlisle station on 5 March 1972 with a Sunday Euston Glasgow train. The scene here will dramatically change in 1976, when the electrification from Crewe to Glasgow takes place.

A rare visit to York by a Class 50 happened occasionally when one had been overhauled at Doncaster Works. The usual way to get it back to its home depot at Plymouth Laira was for it to work the 09.50 Edinburgh–Plymouth train from York, and in this picture No. 55013 *The Black Watch*, which has just arrived from Edinburgh, is about to hand over to No. 50033 *Glorious* for the journey west.

D9006 *The Fife and Fofar Yeomanry* passes Hadley Wood station on 8 February 1969 with an InterCity service from Newcastle to King's Cross.

D9012 *Crepello* causes a mini snowstorm as it speeds through Hadley Wood with the Flying Scotsman on the last part of its journey to King's Cross on 8 February 1969.

D9021 *Argyll and Sutherland Highlander* approaches Potters Bar on 17 February 1969 with the Flying Scotsman for King's Cross.

D9015 *Tulyar* heads north through Harringay West station on 17 February 1969 with the Tees Tyne Pullman. The wonderful array of semaphore signals in this area was swept away during the resignalling in preparation for electrification of the suburban services in the early 1970s.

D9008 *The Green Howards* passes Station Road level crossing and the North Eastern Railway signal box at Warkworth on 10 May 1969 with the Flying Scotsman, heading for Edinburgh.

No. 9020 *Nimbus* passes Hadley Wood with the northbound Yorkshire Pullman on 7 August 1969. At this time the old Pullman car colours of brown and cream were being replaced with the new BR corporate blue and grey livery.

D9004 *Queen's Own Highlander* approaches Hadley Wood north tunnel with the 12.00 express from Edinburgh to King's Cross on 7 August 1969.

Under the watchful eye of a young trainspotter, No. 9009 *Alycidon* departs from York station on 16 September 1972 with the 09.00 King's Cross to Newcastle train.

No. 55001 *St Paddy* makes its only stop at Newcastle station while working the northbound Flying Scotsman on 11 July 1976.

No. 55011 *The Royal Northumberland Fusiliers* crosses the Royal Border Bridge at Berwick-upon-Tweed on 12 July 1976 with the 12.00 King's Cross to Edinburgh service.

No. 55003 *Meld* and No. 55015 *Tulyar* stand at the buffer stops in Platforms 1 and 2 at King's Cross station, having just arrived with expresses from the north in September 1976.

No. 55006 *The Fife and Forfar Yeomanry* makes a smoky departure from King's Cross station with the 11.00 service for Edinburgh in September 1976.

No. 55010 *The King's Own Scottish Borderer* speeds towards King's Cross through Hitchin station with an express from Newcastle in June 1978.

A very down at heel No. 55020 *Nimbus* at the Doncaster open day on 18 June 1978. This locomotive was taken out of service after a major failure and was cannibalised for spare parts, becoming the first Deltic to be broken up in January 1980.

No. 55013 *The Black Watch* calls at York station on a very wet day in April 1979 with a Newcastle to King's Cross train.

No. 55003 *Meld* passes York Clifton with the 07.22 Plymouth to Edinburgh train in April 1979.

No. 55018 *Ballymoss* waits at York station in May 1979 with a southbound additional Saturday-only service.

Seen from a passing train, No. 55003 *Meld* stands at Peterborough TMD in June 1979. No. 55003 was the first Deltic to receive the white surrounds to the cab windows.

No. 55007 *Pinzar* departs from Platform 5 at York station with an express for Edinburgh in October 1979.

No. 55016 *Gordon Highlander* at speed near Tollerton with the 09.50 Edinburgh to Plymouth train in December 1979.

No. 55015 *Tulyar* was the Deltic chosen to take part in the Rainhill Cavalcade on 25 August 1980 and is seen here on a set of container wagons passing the crowded grandstands.

No. 55005 *The Prince of Wales Own Regiment of Yorkshire* heads north at Shipton with the 07.22 Plymouth to Edinburgh train on a dull June day in 1980.

Two views of No. 55002 *The Kings Own Yorkshire Light Infantry* (*KOYLI*). The first shows No. 55002 at York station on 12 December 1980 with the 15.50 departure for King's Cross, making its first journey after it was restored to its original two-tone green livery, and after the announcement that the locomotive would be saved by the NRM. The second shows No. 55002 passing Haxby Gates on its way to Scarborough with a special organised by the NRM, consisting mainly of Pullman cars, on 18 January 1981.

No. 55015 *Tulyar* passes Dringhouses shortly before arriving at York with an InterCity service in May 1981.

A very travel-stained No. 55004 *Queen's Own Highlander* waits in Platform 5 under the magnificent roof at York station in May 1981 with the 10.50 to King's Cross.

At Newcastle Central, No. 47401 is just visible on a train to Liverpool and No. 55014 *The Duke of Wellington's Regiment* is departing with the Edinburgh to Plymouth train on 6 June 1981.

No. 55022 *Royal Scots Grey* speeds south near Benningborough with a set of Mk 1 coaches on a relief train to King's Cross in August 1981.

No. 55002 *Kings Own Yorkshire Light Infantry* passes Tollerton in August 1981 with a Newcastle to Scarborough summer Saturday train.

No. 55017 *The Durham Light Infantry* passes Chaloners Whin with the 15.50 from York to King's Cross in October 1981. This part of the ECML was closed when the Selby bypass was opened in 1983.

No. 55010 *The King's Own Scottish Borderer* has just arrived at King's Cross station in October 1981 with a train from York. A major refurbishment of the station had just been completed and the brickwork looks in excellent condition, considering that the station dates from 1852.

No. 55019 *Royal Highland Fusilier* is at York station, waiting to depart for the carriage sidings with a train just arrived from King's Cross. This photograph was taken in November 1981.

No. 55019 *Royal Highland Fusilier* waits to depart from York station with the evening stopping train to King's Cross in December 1981.

On 2 January 1982, the last Deltic-hauled special train ran from King's Cross to Edinburgh and return. This was the Deltic Scotsman Farewell organised by British Rail Eastern Region, and was hauled by No. 55015 *Tulyar*. These two pictures show the pilot locomotive, No. 55009 *Alycidon*, that ran in advance of the special, and the special itself, both taken just north of York at Clifton. All the way along the ECML, huge crowds of enthusiasts turned out to watch the special pass. The return train hauled by No. 55022 *Royal Scots Grey* ran after dark, so I went down to York station to pay my last respects, and it came through on the middle road with the platforms either side crowded with people from end to end. It was quite a send-off.

The amazing scene at the Doncaster Works Deltic Farewell open day on 27 February 1982, which was attended by thousands of enthusiasts paying their last respects to one of the most popular diesel classes to run on British Rail.

Blue No. 55016 *Gordon Highlander* is in the foreground, with young enthusiasts having a great time cabbing No. 55002 *KOYLI* at the Doncaster Works Deltic Farewell open day. No. 55016 has been saved and is currently in the care of Locomotive Services Limited, and No. 55002 is part of the National Collection at the NRM, York.

No. 55009, seen as it came out of service complete with last special insignia, was one of the six Deltics that survived into preservation, and is in the care of the Deltic Preservation Society.

D9000 *Royal Scots Grey* at York station on 6 June 1997 with Hertfordshire Railtours' The Deltic Scotsman. This was the day of the funeral of Diana, Princess of Wales, hence the wreath on the front of the loco.

No. 9016 *Gordon Highlander* at Doncaster Works open day on 27 July 2003 while under the ownership of Porterbrook and seen here in their purple livery.